MIDGET
Mark III

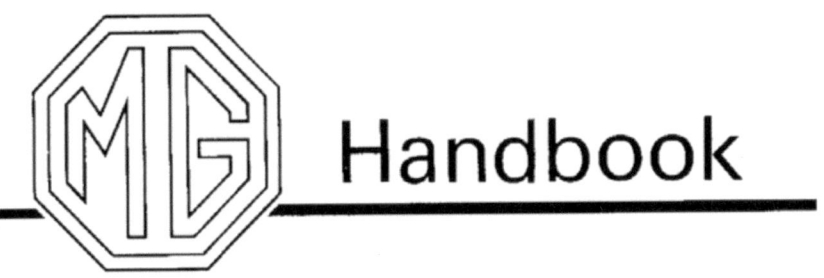

Handbook

Published by
THE M.G. CAR COMPANY LIMITED
Proprietors: Morris Motors Limited

Publication Part No. AKD 4850 © THE BRITISH MOTOR CORPORATION LTD., 1967

FOREWORD

This Handbook provides an introduction to your car and includes information on the necessary care and maintenance required for trouble-free motoring.

Your BMC Distributor or Dealer is provided with the latest information concerning special service tools and workshop techniques. This enables him to undertake your service and repairs in the most efficient and economic manner.

Owners are recommended to use the Maintenance Voucher Scheme. A Passport to Service containing service vouchers is provided and regular use of the vouchers in sequence is the best safeguard against the possibility of abnormal repair bills at a later date. Failure to have your car correctly maintained could invalidate the terms of the Warranty.

Completed voucher counterfoils are proof of regular servicing and could well enhance the value of your vehicle in the eyes of a prospective buyer. A replacement Passport to Service voucher book is obtainable from Distributors or Dealers.

Please note that references to right- or left-hand in this Handbook are made when viewing the car from the rear.

THE M.G. CAR COMPANY LIMITED
Proprietors: Morris Motors Limited

ABINGDON-ON-THAMES
BERKSHIRE, ENGLAND

BMC EXPORT SALES LIMITED
BOX 41 G.P.O.
LONGBRIDGE, BIRMINGHAM

CONTENTS

	Page
Controls	4
Instruments and switches	6
Body fittings	9
Heating and ventilating	14
Cleaning	15
Running instructions	16
Cooling system	19
Wheels/tyres	21
Brakes	24
Electrical	26
Ignition	31
Wiring diagram	34
Engine	36
Gearbox/rear axle	41
Steering/suspension	42
General data	44
Maintenance summary	46
BMC Service	48
Lubrication	50
Recommended lubricants	52

CONTROLS

Fig. 1 Left-hand drive

Fig. 2 Right-hand drive

(1) **Direction indicator switch.** The switch is self-cancelling and operates the indicators only when the ignition is switched on.

(1) *(optional extra)* **Headlight flasher.** The switch is integral with the direction indicator switch and flashes the headlights when the switch lever is lifted towards the steering-wheel.

(2) **Headlight beam dipping switch.** The switch lowers the beams on one application and raises them on the next. A warning light (see page 7) will glow when the beams are in the raised position.

(3) (4) (5) **Pedals.** The pedals are arranged in the conventional positions.

The brake pedal operates the brake hydraulic system and applies the brakes on all four wheels, also bringing the stop warning lights into operation when the ignition is switched on.

Fig. 1

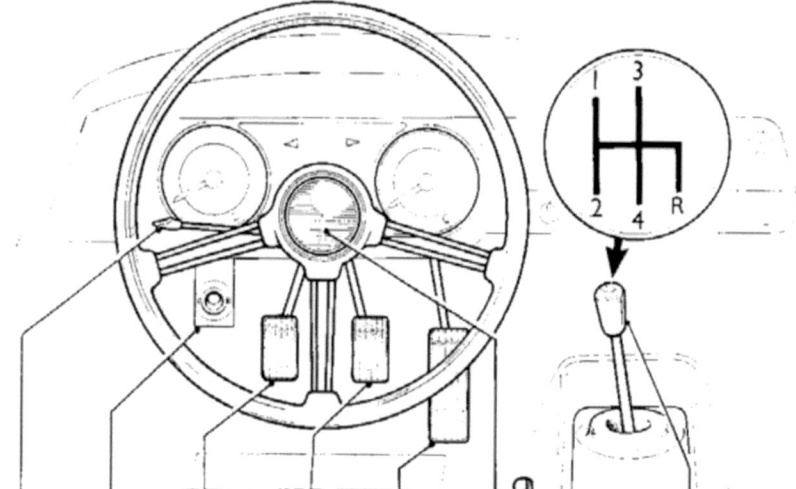

(6) **Horn switch.** The horn is sounded by pressing the centre disc of the steering-wheel.

(7) **Hand brake.** The hand brake is of the pull-up lever type, operating mechanically on the rear wheels only. To release the hand brake pull the lever upwards slightly, depress the button on the end of the lever and push the lever down.

(8) **Gear lever.** The gear positions are indicated on the lever knob. To engage reverse gear move the lever to the right in the neutral position until resistance is felt, apply further side pressure to overcome the resistance and then move it backwards to engage the gear. Synchromesh is provided on second, third, and fourth gears.

Fig. 2

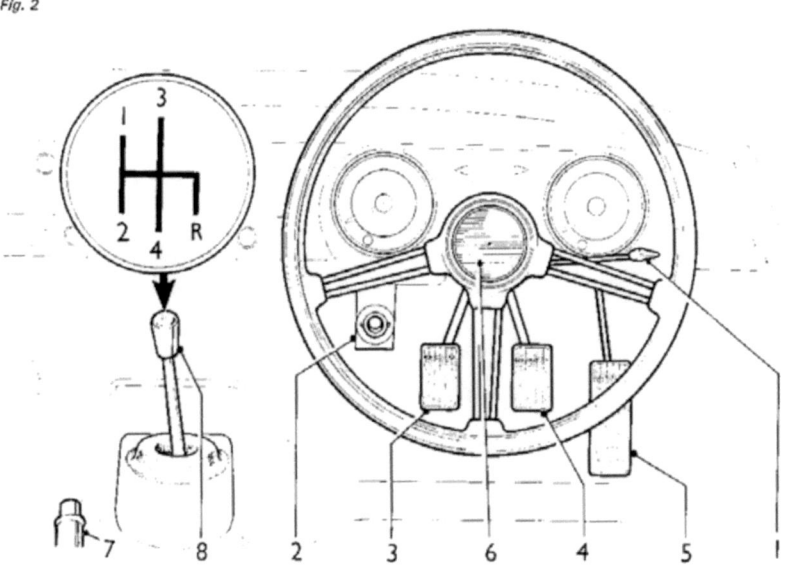

INSTRUMENTS AND SWITCHES

Fig. 1 Left-hand drive

Fig. 2 Right-hand drive

(2) **Speedometer.** In addition to indicating the road speed this instrument also records the total distance (10) and the distance travelled for any particular trip (1). To reset the trip recorder, push the knob (12) upwards and turn it clockwise: it is important that all the counters are returned to zero.

(3) **Direction indicator warning light (green).** The arrow-shaped lights show the direction selected and operate with the flashing direction indicators.

(4) **Tachometer.** This instrument indicates the revolutions per minute of the engine and assists the driver to use the most effective engine speed range for maximum performance in any gear (see page 18).

(5) **Lighting switch.** Move the lever downwards to the first position to switch on the side and tail lights, and into the fully down position to operate the headlights.

(6) **Fuel gauge.** When the ignition is switched on the fuel gauge indicates approximately the amount of fuel in the tank. An important note on filling with fuel is given on page 16.

(7) **Ignition and starter switch.** The ignition and starter are both controlled by a single switch operated by a removable key. To switch on the ignition insert the key and turn it in a clockwise direction until a slight resistance is felt. Further movement in the same direction operates the starter motor. Release the key immediately the engine starts.

To reduce the possibility of theft ignition switches are **not** marked with a number. Owners are advised to make a note of the number stamped on their ignition key.

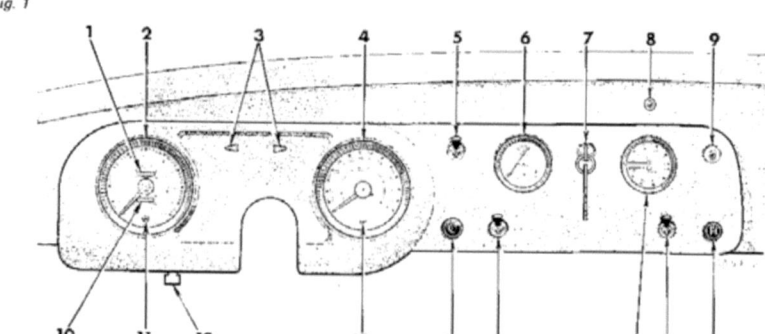

Fig. 1

(8) **Oil filter warning light (amber).** The warning light indicates the need to change the oil filter element and engine oil (see page 18).

(9) **Windscreen washer.** To wash the windscreen press the control knob. When following other vehicles, particularly under dirty road conditions, the washer should be operated before the wiper blades are set in motion.

In cold weather the reservoir should be filled with a mixture of water and recommended washer solvent to prevent the water freezing in the reservoir and on the windscreen.

Do not use radiator anti-freeze solution in the windscreen washer.

(11) **Headlight main-beam warning light (blue).** The light glows when the headlights are switched on and the beam is in the raised position. The light goes out when the beam is dipped.

(13) **Ignition warning light (red).** The ignition warning light serves the dual purpose of reminding the driver to switch off the ignition, and of acting as a no-charge indicator (see page 17).

(14) **Mixture control (choke).** Pull out the knob marked 'C' to enrich the fuel/air mixture to assist starting when the engine is cold. Notes on setting the control are given on page 17.

(15) **Windscreen wiper switch.** Move the switch lever down to bring both wiper blades into operation. The blades park automatically when the lever is raised to the off position.

(16) **Oil pressure gauge.** The gauge registers the pressure of the oil in the engine lubrication system. Important notes on its indications are given on page 17.

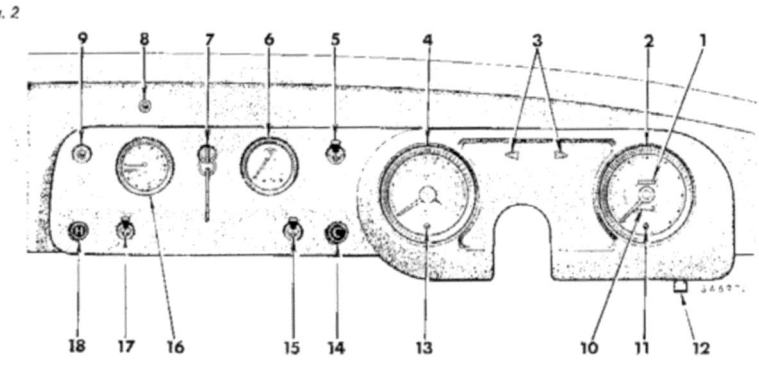

Fig. 2

Instruments and Switches

(16) **Coolant temperature gauge.** The gauge indicates the temperature of the coolant as it leaves the engine cylinder head. An important note about temperature is on page 18.

(17) **Panel light switch.** This is a lever-type switch. The panel lights will only function when the sidelights are switched on.

(18) **Blower and ventilating control.** This is a dual control for the ventilation blower
(*optional extra*) and air intake.

Full operating instructions are given on page 14.

BODY FITTINGS

Seat adjustment
Fig. 1

Both seats are adjustable and can be moved easily into the most comfortable position. Push the lever located beneath the front of the seat to the left to unlock the driver's seat and to the right to unlock the passenger's seat; hold the lever in this position while the seat position is adjusted. The locking pin is spring-loaded and will automatically lock the seat in the required position when the lever is released.

Seat belts
Fig. 2

Seat belts are obtainable from authorized Distributors and Dealers, and should only be fitted by them to the attachment points incorporated in the body structure.

The approved 'Kangol Magnet' belts consist of a long belt attached at one end to the rear wheel arch and the other end to the sill, and a short belt attached to the wearer's side of the drive shaft tunnel.

To fasten, lift the magnetic buckle tongue and engage the hook with the hinged part of the tongue.

To release, lift the magnetic buckle tongue.

To adjust, tighten the short belt with the adjuster at the buckle until the buckle rests on the side of the hip. With the adjuster at the sill tighten the belt until lap belt fits comfortably and there is just room to pass a hand between the diagonal belt and the chest. Slight readjustment may be necessary during use.

To stow, hook the buckle on the long belt into the slot in the bracket provided on the hood hinge plate, and attach the magnetic buckle on the short belt to the seat frame.

Windows and ventilators

Rotate the handle on each door to open and close the windows.

The ventilation panels adjacent to each window may be opened after releasing the catch.

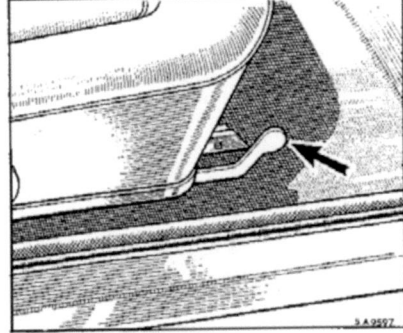

Fig. 1

Fig. 2

Body Fittings

Door locks
Fig. 3
Both doors may be locked from the outside with the ignition key. Turn the key clockwise to lock the doors and anti-clockwise to unlock. After locking or unlocking the doors return the key to the vertical position to withdraw it.

The passenger door may be locked from inside the car by turning the locking knob downwards. Turn the knob upwards to unlock the door.

Luggage compartment
Fig. 4
To open, turn the handle in an anti-clockwise direction and raise the lid. Unclip the stay under the lid and secure the free end in the bracket attached to the side of the luggage compartment. When closed, turn the handle clockwise; the compartment may then be locked with the key provided.

Bonnet
Fig. 5
To open the bonnet, pull the release inside the car and push the safety catch backwards. Release the bonnet stay from its clip and place the free end in the bracket attached to the front wheel arch.

To close, secure the stay in its clip and lower the bonnet. Apply light pressure with the palms of the hands at the front corners of the bonnet and press down quickly. The safety catch and lock will be heard to engage.

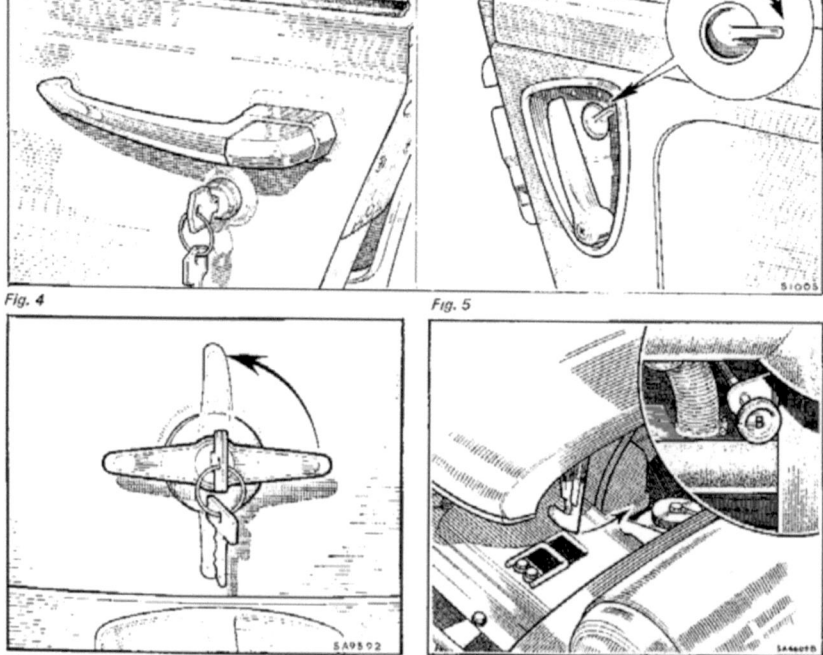

Fig. 3

Fig. 4

Fig. 5

Hood It is most important that the instructions given for raising, lowering, or folding the hood are followed; do not apply pressure to the frame-members other than the header rail, undue force is not necessary and should be avoided. Do not fold or stow the hood when it is wet or damp.

Lowering. Release the press studs on the windscreen frame and hood hinge links (see Fig. 6). Open the toggle catches on the windscreen rail (inset Fig. 6).

Release the four lift-dot fasteners from each rear quarter panel. Press the hood header rail rearwards, at the same time keeping the hood material pulled out towards the rear away from the frame (Fig. 7).

Collapse the frame into its stowage position and lay the hood material on the luggage compartment lid. Fold the quarter-lights inwards, on a line between the quarter-light and back-light (Fig. 8), then fold the hood over the frame into the rear compartment (Fig. 9).

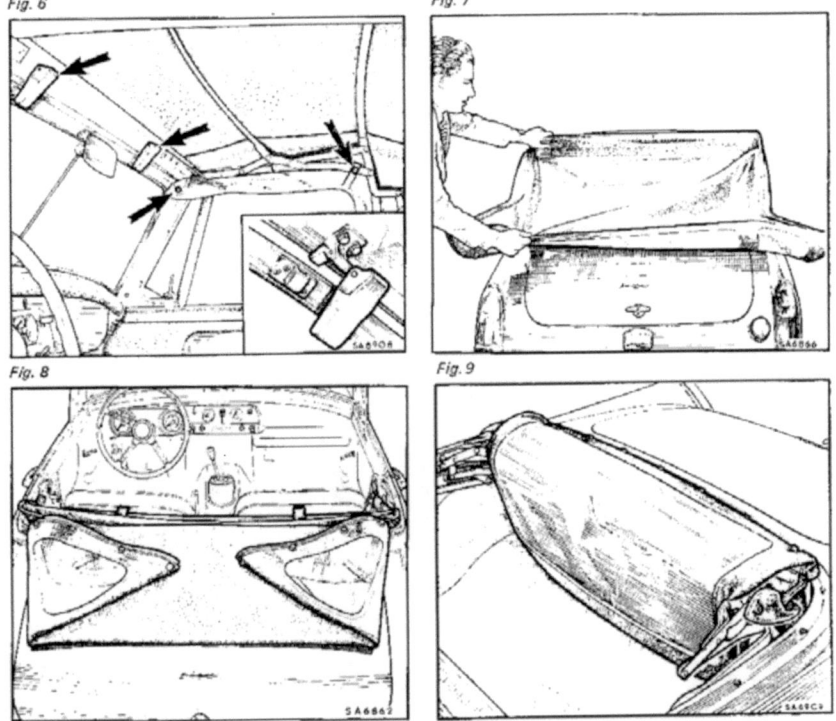

Fig. 6

Fig. 7

Fig. 8

Fig. 9

Body Fittings

Lay the hood cover over the hood and secure the rear edge with the lift-dot fasteners. Arrange the cover and secure it at the sides with the fasteners provided on each quarter panel. Secure the front edge to the cockpit rear panel with the four press studs (see Fig. 10).

Raising. Remove the hood cover and open both doors. Lift the hood material over the frame and lay it on the luggage compartment lid. Unfold the quarter-lights and pull the header rail forwards and upwards at the point indicated by the label. Ensure that the material takes up its correct position as the frame is erected.

Engage the hood toggle fastener tongues in their sockets on the windscreen rail, check that the rubber sealing strip is correctly positioned forward of the rail, and fasten the toggle links.

Secure the hood with the fasteners on the rear quarter panels, windscreen sideposts, and frame hinge links. Stow the hood cover.

Tonneau cover *(optional extra)* *Fitting*. Assemble the tonneau rail and fit it into the slots of the brackets provided on the hood frame hinge plates.

Lay the cover over the cockpit and secure the rear edge and sides with the fasteners on the tonneau and quarter-panels.

Extend the cover forward and secure the front edge to the fasteners on the fascia panel top.

Usage. The centre zip allows the cover to be folded down to give access to the driving seat or both seats. Fold the cover down behind the seat and secure it with the fasteners to the heelboard (see Fig. 11). The short side zips permit the use of seat belts when the cover is folded down.

Removing. Reverse the fitting procedure.

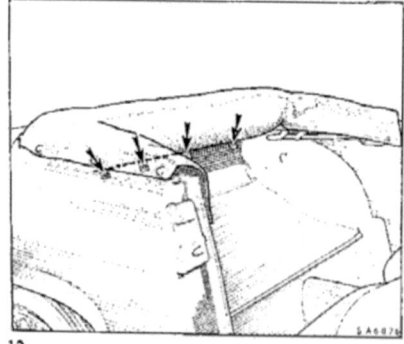

Fig. 10

Fig. 11

Hard top
(optional
extra) *Fitting.* Lower the hood and fit the hard top hood cover.

Position the hard top on the car and engage the toggle fastener tongues in their sockets on the windscreen rail. Check that the rubber sealing strip is correctly positioned forward of the rail. Fasten the toggle links and lock them with the securing brackets (inset, Fig. 12). Fit the bolts into both side-fixing brackets and tighten them down gently and evenly until the hard top seals at both sides and the rear. Do not tighten the bolts hard down.

Check the width of the gap between the flanges of the side-fixing brackets (see Fig. 13), remove the bolts and fit packing washers between the flanges to the thickness of the gap.

Refit and tighten the securing bolts.

Fig. 12

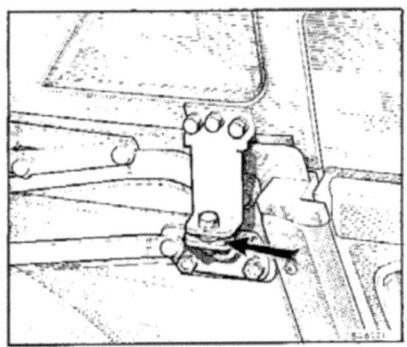

Fig. 13

HEATING AND VENTILATING

Fresh-air heater (*optional extra*) The heating and ventilating system is designed to provide fresh-air, either heated by the engine cooling system or at outside air temperature, to the car at floor level and, for demisting and defrosting, to the windscreen.

Air enters through a forward-facing intake; the ram effect caused by the car's motion provides air for the heater's requirements at speeds above 25 m.p.h. (40 km.p.h.). A blower motor is provided for use at lower speeds or when a greater quantity of air is required.

Air distribution Two doors, located one at each side of the gearbox tunnel, control distribution of air between screen and car interior. To supply air to the car, open the doors; to boost the flow of air to the screen, close the doors.

Heater control valve *Fig. 1* A valve controlling the flow of hot water through the heater unit is fitted at the rear of the cylinder head. The valve is opened by turning it in an anti-clockwise direction when heating is required or shut off by turning clockwise when the system is to be used for cool air ventilation.

Air-intake control *Fig. 2* The knob 'H' on the fascia panel controls the booster blower motor and also a shut-off valve incorporated in the air intake. This valve prevents fumes entering the car when driving in heavy traffic.

To switch on the blower, turn the knob in a clockwise direction.

To close the shut-off valve, switch off the blower and pull out the knob. The blower motor cannot be switched on again until the shut-off valve is returned to the open position.

Fresh-air unit (*optional extra*) This unit is similar to the fresh-air heater except that the air supplied to the car is not heated. The air intake is controlled by a knob 'A' on the fascia panel which functions in the same way as that supplied with the heater unit.

Fig. 1

Fig. 2

CLEANING

Coachwork Regular care of the body finish is necessary if the new appearance of the car exterior is to be maintained against the effects of air pollution, rain, and mud.

Wash the bodywork frequently, using a soft sponge and plenty of water containing a mild detergent. Large deposits of mud must be softened with water before using the sponge. Smears should be removed by a second wash in clean water, and with the sponge if necessary. When dry, clean the surface of the car with a damp chamois-leather. In addition to the regular maintenance, special attention is required if the car is driven in extreme conditions such as sea spray, or on salted roads. In these conditions and with other forms of severe contamination an additional washing operation is necessary, which should include underbody hosing. Any damaged areas should be immediately covered with paint and a complete repair effected as soon as possible. Before touching-in light scratches and abrasions with paint thoroughly clean the surface. Use petrol/white spirit (gasoline/hydrocarbon solvent) to remove spots of tar or grease.

The application of BMC Car Polish is all that is required to remove traffic film and to ensure the retention of the new appearance.

Bright trim Never use an abrasive on stainless, chromium, aluminium, or plastic bright parts and on no account clean them with metal polish. Remove spots of grease or tar with petrol/white spirit (gasoline/hydrocarbon solvent) and wash frequently with water containing a mild detergent. When the dirt has been removed polish with a clean dry cloth or chamois-leather until bright. Any slight tarnish found on stainless or plated parts which have not received regular washing may be removed with BMC Chrome Cleaner. An occasional application of mineral light oil or grease will help to preserve the finish, particularly during winter when salt may be used on the roads, but these protectives must not be applied to plastic finishes.

Windscreen If windscreen smearing has occurred, it can be removed with BMC Screen Cleaner.

Interior Clean the carpets with a stiff brush or vacuum cleaner, preferably before washing the outside of the car. The most satisfactory way to give carpets a thorough cleaning is to apply BMC 2-way Cleaner with a semi-stiff brush, brush vigorously, and remove the surplus with a damp cloth or sponge. Carpets should not be cleaned by the 'dry-clean' process. The upholstery may be treated with BMC 2-way Cleaner applied with a damp cloth and a light rubbing action. A razor blade will remove transfers from the window glass.

Hood To clean the hood it is only necessary to use soap and water, with a soft brush to remove any ingrained dirt. Frequent washing with soap and water considerably improves the appearance and wearing qualities of the hood, and it should be washed at least as often as the rest of the car.

Do not use caustic soaps, detergents, or spirit cleaners to clean the hood or the hood back-light.

The BMC approved products mentioned above are obtainable from your Distributor or Dealer.

RUNNING INSTRUCTIONS

High-compression engine (8·8:1) — This engine is a highly developed unit and, as such, specialized maintenance is required to maintain it at the peak of its mechanical efficiency. Recommendations on the sparking plugs, ignition settings, and fuel to be used, are given and it is stressed that failures are bound to occur if these are not strictly adhered to. Particular care is needed owing to the high compression ratio of the engine which makes it extremely sensitive to variations in fuel, ignition timing, and heat range of the sparking plugs.

The range of fuels, sparking plugs, and ignition settings is narrower than those required with lower compression engines and it is essential that the mixture should always be correct, particularly never over-weak at maximum load or power.

High-compression engines are very sensitive to variations in spark advance (over-advance) and to fuel/air ratio (mixture). Variation in these settings will increase the combustion temperature, and if the variation is excessive pre-ignition will cause high shock waves resulting in damage to the engine.

The engine should be decarbonized at regular intervals as excessive deposits of ash in the combustion chambers can cause pre-ignition difficulties.

Choice of fuel H.C. engine — The octane number of a motor fuel is an indication given by the fuel technicians of its knock resistance (pinking). High-octane fuels have been produced to improve the efficiency of engines by allowing them to operate on high compression ratios, resulting in better fuel economy and greater power. Owing to the high compression ratio of the engine, fuels with an octane rating below 94 are not suitable. Should it be necessary to use a fuel with a lower octane number, the car must be used very carefully until the correct fuel can be obtained.

It is necessary to use Premium grade fuels with octane ratings of 97 to 99 when optimum performance is required.

Filling up with fuel — When filling up with fuel avoid filling the tank until fuel is visible in the filler intake tube. Should this be done and the car left in the sun, there will be a considerable risk of fuel leakage due to expansion, and consequent danger from exposed fuel. If inadvertently overfilled and the car is to be parked, take care to park it in the shade with the filler intake as high as possible.

Starting — Check that the gear lever is in the neutral position.

If the engine is cold, pull out the mixture control (choke). In extremely cold conditions it may be necessary to pull the control out to its fullest extent.

Switch on the ignition, check that the ignition warning light glows and that the fuel gauge registers, then operate the starter.

As soon as the engine starts, release the ignition key and warm up the engine at a fairly fast speed (see **'Warming up'**). Check that the oil pressure gauge is registering and that the ignition warning light has gone out. Push in the mixture control (choke) completely as soon as the engine will run evenly without its use.

Starter Do not operate the starter for longer than 5 to 6 seconds.

Wait until the crankshaft has stopped turning before using the starter again.

If after a reasonable number of attempts the engine should fail to start, switch off the ignition and investigate the cause. Continued use of the starter when the engine will not start, not only discharges the battery but may also damage the starter.

If the starter pinion fails to engage with the flywheel ring, or fails to disengage when the engine starts, the starter will emit a high-pitched whine; release the ignition key immediately.

Should the starter pinion become jammed in mesh with the flywheel ring, turn the squared end of the armature spindle with a spanner.

Mixture control (choke) Always use the minimum setting for the shortest possible time.

As soon as possible after the engine has started, push the control completely home.

To obtain a fast engine idling speed, set the control to within the first ¼ in. (6 mm.) approx. of its initial movement.

Ignition warning light The light should glow when the ignition is switched on, and go out and stay out at all times while the engine is running above normal idling speed. Failure to do so indicates a fault in the battery charging system. Check that the fan belt is correctly tensioned before consulting your Distributor or Dealer.

Oil pressure gauge The gauge should register a pressure as soon as the engine is started up. The pressure may rise above 70 lb./sq. in. (4·92 kg./cm.^{2}) when the engine is started from cold and as the oil is circulated and warmed the pressure should then drop to between 40 and 70 lb./sq. in. (2·81 to 4·92 kg./cm.^{2}) at normal running speeds and to approximately 20 lb./sq. in. (1·4 kg /cm.^{2}) at idling speed.

Should the gauge fail to register any pressure, stop the engine immediately and investigate the cause. Start by checking the oil level.

Warming up Research has proved that the practice of warming up an engine by allowing it to idle slowly is definitely harmful. The correct procedure is to let the engine run fairly fast, approximately 1,000 r.p.m., corresponding to a speed of about 15 m.p.h. (24 km.p.h.) in top gear, so that it attains its correct working temperature as quickly as possible. Allowing the engine to work slowly in a cold state leads to excessive cylinder wear, and far less damage is done by driving the car straight on to the road from cold than by letting the engine idle slowly in the garage.

Running Instructions

Temperature gauge   When the engine is running the gauge indicates the temperature of the coolant leaving the cylinder head.

As overheating may cause serious damage, the readings should be noted and after the initial rise in temperature during the warming up period any sudden upward change in the reading calls for immediate investigation.

When the ignition is switched off the needle returns to the 'cold' position.

Running in   The treatment given to a new car will have an important bearing on its subsequent life, and engine speeds during this early period must be limited. The following instructions should be strictly adhered to.
During the first 500 miles (800 km.)
DO NOT exceed 45 m.p.h. (72 km.p.h.).
DO NOT operate at full throttle in any gear.
DO NOT allow the engine to labour in any gear.

Tachometer   For normal road work, and to obtain the most satisfactory service from your engine, select the appropriate gear to maintain engine speeds of between 2,000 and 4,500 r.p.m.

When maximum acceleration is required upward gear selections should be made when the needle reaches the yellow sector (5,500–6,000 r.p.m.). Prolonged or excessive use of the highest engine speeds will tend to shorten the life of the engine. Allowing the engine to pull hard at low engine speeds must be avoided as this also has a detrimental effect on the engine.

The beginning of the red sector (6,000 r.p.m.) indicates the maximum safe speed for the engine.

Never allow the needle to enter the red sector.

Oil filter warning light   If the light comes on and continues to glow when the engine is running, the need for a new oil filter element and a change of engine oil is indicated; this should be carried out as soon as possible within a maximum of a further 300 miles (500 km.).

If 6,000 miles (10000 km.) or six months have passed since the last oil and filter element change, although the warning light has not come on, both engine oil and filter element must be changed.

Wet brakes   When the vehicle is being washed or driven through water the brake linings may become wet. To dry them, apply the brakes several times with the vehicle moving slowly. Driving with wet brakes is very dangerous.

Towing   Should it become necessary to tow the car, use the towing eyes provided.

COOLING SYSTEM

Radiator filler cap (3) The system is pressurized to 7 lb./sq. in. (·5 kg./cm.²) when hot, and the pressure must be released gradually when the filler cap is removed. It is advisable to protect the hands against escaping steam and turn the cap slowly anti-clockwise until the resistance of the safety stops is felt. Leave the cap in this position until all pressure is released. Press the cap downwards against the spring to clear the safety stops, and continue turning until it can be lifted off.

Draining the cooling system There are two draining points for the system, a plug (1) on the cylinder block, and a tap (2) on the radiator bottom tank. To drain the coolant stand the car on level ground, remove the radiator filler cap, open the radiator tap, and remove the cylinder block plug.

When draining in freezing weather, do so when the engine is hot. Run the engine slowly for one minute when the water has ceased flowing to clear any water from the pump and other places where it might collect. Finally, leave a reminder on the vehicle to the effect that the cooling system has been drained.

If the system contains anti-freeze remember to collect it in a clean container for future use.

Filling the cooling system To avoid wastage by overflow add just sufficient coolant to cover the bottom of the header tank. Run the engine until it is hot and add sufficient coolant to bring the surface to the level of the indicator positioned inside the header tank below the filler neck.

NOTE.—If a heater is fitted ensure that the water valve on the cylinder head is set to the 'open' position when draining or filling the system.

Fig. 1

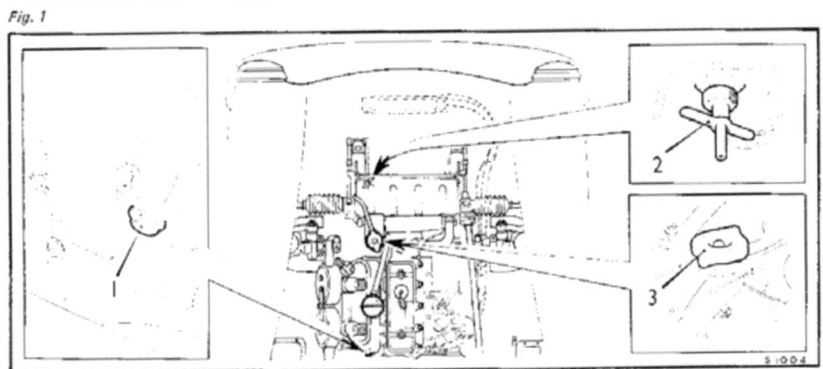

Cooling System

Frost precautions Water, when it freezes, expands, and if precautions are not taken there is considerable risk of bursting the radiator, cylinder block, or heater (where fitted). Such damage may be avoided by draining the cooling system when the car is left for any length of time in frosty weather, or by adding anti-freeze to the water.

Warning.—When a heater unit is fitted an anti-freeze solution must be added in the cooling system since no provision is made for draining the heater.

Do not use radiator anti-freeze solution in the windscreen washer.

Anti-freeze solutions Before adding anti-freeze mixture to the radiator it is advisable to clean out the cooling system thoroughly by flushing out the passages with a hose inserted in the filler hole while keeping both drain points open.

Only top up when the cooling system is at its normal running temperature in order to avoid losing anti-freeze due to expansion.

Make sure that the cooling system is water-tight, examine all joints, and replace any defective rubber hose with new.

Anti-freeze can remain in the cooling system for two years provided that the specific gravity of the coolant is checked periodically and anti-freeze added as necessary. This operation should be carried out by an authorized Distributor or Dealer.

After the second winter the system should be drained and refilled with fresh water, and the appropriate amount of anti-freeze added when required.

Only anti-freeze of the ethylene glycol or glycerine type is suitable for use in the cooling system. We recommend owners to use Bluecol Anti-freeze (non-corrosive) in order to protect the cooling system during frosty weather and reduce corrosion to a minimum. We also approve the use of any anti-freeze which conforms to Specification B.S.3151 or B.S.3152.

The correct quantities of anti-freeze for different degrees of frost protection are:

Anti-freeze	Commences to freeze		Frozen solid		Amount of anti-freeze		
%	°C.	°F.	°C.	°F.	Pts.	U.S. Pts.	Litres
25	−13	9	−26	−15	$2\frac{3}{4}$	3	1·5
$33\frac{1}{3}$	−19	−2	−36	−33	$3\frac{1}{2}$	4	2
50	−36	−33	−48	−53	$5\frac{1}{4}$	6	3

WHEELS/TYRES

Jacking up
Fig. 1
The jack is designed to lift one side of the car at a time. Apply the hand brake, and place a wedge against each side of one of the wheels on the opposite side of the car to the one being jacked.

Remove the plug from the jacking socket located in the door sill panel and insert the lifting arm of the jack into the socket. Make **certain that the jack lifting arm is pushed fully into the socket and that the base of the jack is on firm ground.** The jack should lean slightly outwards at the top to allow for the radial movement of the car as it is raised.

Jack maintenance
If the jack is neglected it may be difficult to use in a roadside emergency. Examine it occasionally, clean off accumulated dust, and lightly oil the thread to prevent the formation of rust.

WHEELS
Pressed type
Removing the wheel discs
Fig. 2
Insert the wheel disc lever in the recess provided in the road wheel and lever off the disc, using a sideways motion.

To refit the hub disc place the rim over two of the buttons on the wheel centre and give the outer face a sharp blow with the hand over the third button.

Removing and refitting
Fig. 3
(1)
Slacken the four nuts securing the road wheel to the hub; turn anti-clockwise to loosen and clockwise to tighten. Raise the car with the jack to lift the wheel clear of the ground and remove the nuts. Withdraw the road wheel from the hub. When refitting the road wheel locate the wheel on the hub, lightly tighten the nuts with the wheel nut spanner (securing nuts must be fitted with the **taper side towards the wheel**), and lower the jack. Fully tighten the wheel nuts, tightening them diagonally and progressively, at the same time avoid over-tightening.

Replace the wheel disc and jack socket plug.

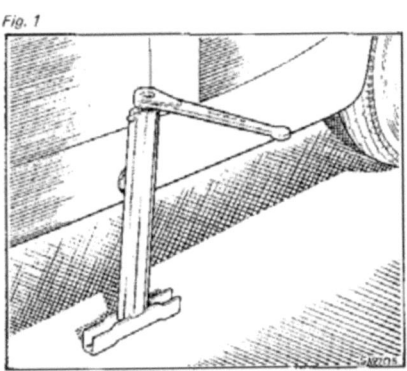
Fig. 1

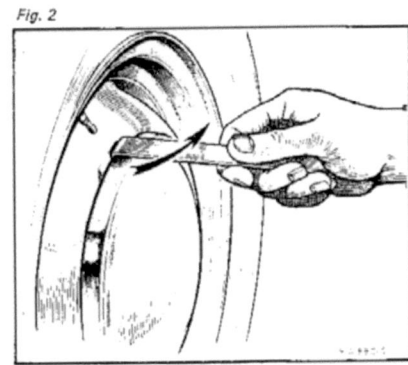
Fig. 2

Wheels/Tyres

Wire type
Removing and refitting
Fig. 3 (2)

Use the mallet to slacken the winged hub nut or the spanner to slacken the octagonal hub nut used.

Always jack up a wheel before using the hammer, and always hammer the nuts tight.

Locknuts are marked 'LEFT' or 'RIGHT' to show to which side of the car they must be fitted, and also with the word 'UNDO' and an arrow.

Before replacing a wheel wipe all serrations, threads, and cones of the wheel and hub and then lightly coat them with grease. If a forced change is made on the road, remove, clean, and grease as soon as convenient.

Maintenance

When the car is new, after the first long run or after 50 miles (80 km.) of short runs, jack up the wheels and hammer the nuts to make sure that they are tight.

Once a year remove the wheels for examination and regreasing.

Tyre maintenance
Fig. 4

To obtain the best tyre mileage and to suppress the development of irregular wear on the tyres the wheels can be interchanged diagonally bringing the spare wheel into use (see **Radial-ply tyres (SP)**).

Excessive local distortion as a result of striking a kerb, a loose brick, a deep pot-hole, etc., may cause the casing cords to fracture.

Tyres, including the spare, must be maintained at the pressures recommended (see **'GENERAL DATA'**); check with an accurate tyre gauge at least once a week, and regulate as necessary. Pressures should be checked when the tyres are cold; do not reduce the pressure in warm tyres where the increase above the normal pressure is due to temperature.

See that the valve caps are screwed down firmly by hand. The cap prevents the entry of dirt into the valve mechanism and forms an additional seal on the valve, preventing any leakage if the valve core is damaged.

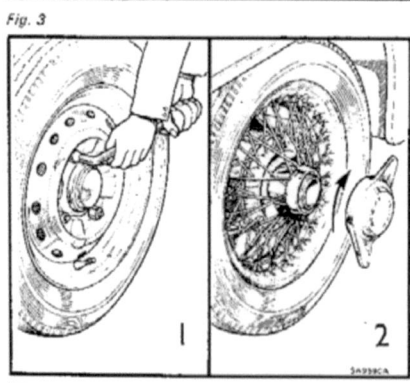

Fig. 3

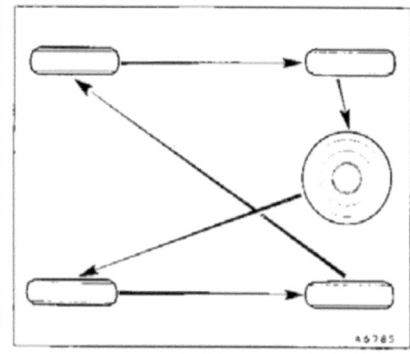

Fig. 4

Flints and other sharp objects should be removed with a penknife or similar tool. If neglected, they may work through the cover.

Any oil or grease which may get onto the tyres should be cleaned off by using fuel sparingly. Do not use paraffin (kerosene), which has a detrimental effect on rubber.

With tubeless tyres penetration does not normally result in deflation and the tyres should be repaired when convenient. Penetrations by objects of small diameter can be repaired with the tyre manufacturer's plugging kit, while more extensive damage requires the removal of the tyre for vulcanizing.

When repairing tubes have punctures or injuries vulcanized. Ordinary patches should only be used for emergencies.

Vulcanizing is absolutely essential in the case of tubes manufactured from synthetic rubber.

Radial-ply tyres (SP) Radial-ply tyres (SP) should only be fitted in sets of four, although in certain circumstances it is permissible to fit a pair on the rear wheels; tyres of different construction must not be used on the same axle. A pair must never be fitted to the front wheels with conventional tyres at the rear. Consult your Distributor or Dealer before changing to radial-ply tyres.

The positional changing of wheels must not be undertaken if radial-ply tyres have been fitted to the rear wheels only.

Wheel and tyre balancing Unbalanced wheel and tyre assemblies may be responsible for abnormal wear of the tyres and vibration in the steering. Consult your Distributor/Dealer.

BRAKES

Brake and clutch master cylinder
Fig. 1

To check the level of the fluid in the brake (1) and clutch (2) master cylinder reservoirs, remove the plastic filler caps.

The fluid level must be maintained at the bottom of the filler neck; use only LOCKHEED DISC BRAKE FLUID (Series II) for topping up. Before refitting the caps, check that the breather holes (indicated by the arrows) are clear.

Rear brakes

Excessive brake pedal travel is an indication that the rear brake-shoes require adjusting. The brakes on both rear wheels must be adjusted to regain even and efficient braking.

Adjusting
Fig. 2

Block the front wheels, fully release the hand brake and jack up each rear wheel in turn. Turn the adjuster (arrowed) in a clockwise direction (viewed from the centre of the car) until the wheel is locked, then turn the adjuster back until the wheel is free to rotate without the shoes rubbing. Repeat the adjustment on the other rear brake.

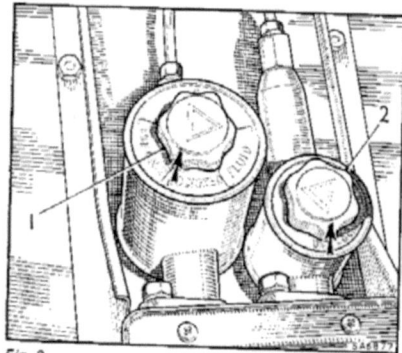

Fig. 1

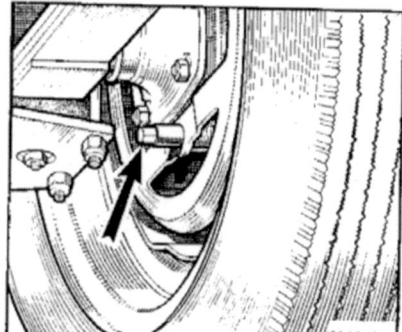

Fig. 2

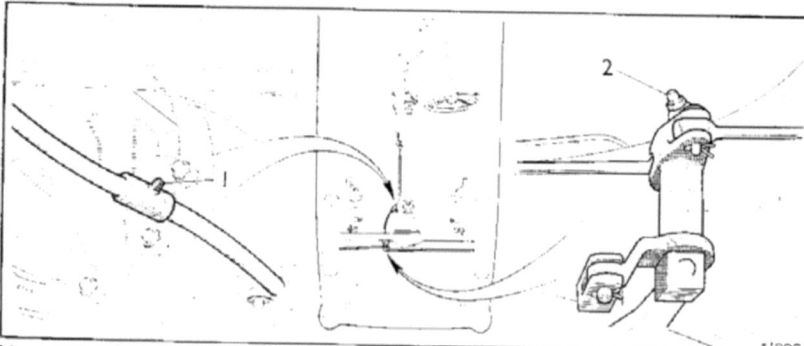

Fig. 3

Front brakes — Wear of the disc brake friction pads is automatically compensated for and manual adjustment is therefore not required. When the lining material has worn down to the minimum permissible thickness of $\frac{1}{16}$ in. (1·6 mm.) the brake pads must be renewed.

Special equipment is required, and new pads should be fitted by an authorized Distributor or Dealer.

Hand brake — The hand brake is automatically adjusted with the rear brakes. If there is excessive movement of the hand brake lever, consult your Distributor or Dealer.

Lubrication
Fig. 3 — Charge the nipples on the hand brake balance lever (2) and hand brake cable (1) with one of the recommended greases.

Preventive maintenance — In addition to the recommended periodical inspection of brake components it is advisable as the car ages, and as a precaution against the effects of wear and deterioration, to make a more searching inspection and renew parts as necessary.

It is recommended that:
(1) Disc brake pads, drum brake linings, hoses, and pipes should be examined at intervals no greater than those laid down in the Passport to Service.
(2) Brake fluid should be changed completely every 18 months or 24,000 miles (40000 km.) whichever is the sooner.
(3) All fluid seals in the hydraulic system and all flexible hoses should be examined and renewed if necessary every 3 years or 40,000 miles (65000 km.) whichever is the sooner. At the same time the working surface of the pistons and of the bores of the master cylinder, wheel cylinders, and other slave cylinders should be examined and new parts fitted where necessary.

Care must be taken always to observe the following points:
(a) At all times use the recommended brake fluid.
(b) Never leave fluid in unsealed containers. It absorbs moisture quickly and this can be dangerous.
(c) Fluid drained from the system or used for bleeding is best discarded.
(d) The necessity for absolute cleanliness throughout cannot be over-emphasized.

ELECTRICAL

Battery The battery electrolyte must be maintained at the correct level.
Fig. 1

Remove the manifold (1) weekly and examine the level of the electrolyte in each cell. If necessary, add sufficient distilled water until the perforated separator guard (2) in each cell is just covered. Do not overfill. More frequent topping up may be necessary in hot climates or if long daily runs are made.

Do not use tap-water and do not use a naked light when examining the condition of the cells. Wipe away all dirt and moisture from the top of the battery.

Never leave the battery in a discharged condition for any length of time. Have it fully charged, and every fortnight give it a short refreshing charge to prevent any tendency for the plates to become permanently sulphated.

Voltage regulator This is a sealed unit (1), located on the right-hand side of the engine bulkhead under the bonnet, controlling the charging rate of the dynamo in accordance with the needs of the battery. The regulator requires no attention and should not be disturbed.
Fig. 2

Fuses The fuses are housed in a separate fuse block (3) on the engine bulkhead.
Fig. 2

The fuse (4) connecting terminals 'A1' and 'A2' protects the accessories that operate irrespective of whether the ignition is on or off.

The fuse (2) connecting terminals 'A3' and 'A4' protects the accessories that operate only when the ignition is switched on (stop lights, direction indicators, etc.).

Blown fuses The units which are protected by the fuses can readily be identified on the wiring diagram. A blown fuse is indicated by the failure of all the units protected by it, and is confirmed by examination of the fuse when withdrawn.

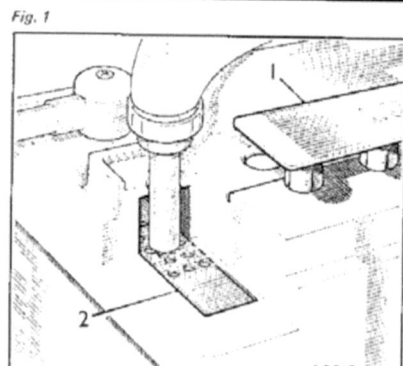

Fig. 1

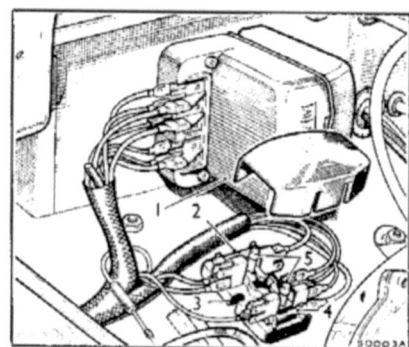

Fig. 2

Before renewing a blown fuse inspect the wiring of the units that have failed for evidence of a short circuit or other fault.

Spare fuses (5) are provided and it is important to use only the correct replacement fuse. The fusing value is marked on a coloured paper slip inside the glass tube of the fuse.

Fuel pump Fuel is delivered to the carburetters by an S.U. electric fuel pump. The pump is situated beneath the luggage compartment on the right-hand side.

Windscreen wiper
Fig. 3
To reposition a wiper arm on the spindle, the arm can be withdrawn when the small spring clip (1) is held clear of the retaining groove. Replace the arm in the required position and push it hard down onto the spindle (2) until it is secured in position by the retaining clip.

To renew a wiper blade pull the wiper arm away from the windscreen and withdraw the blade from the arm with a gentle outward curving pull. Insert the end of the curved 'wrist' of the arm into the slotted spring fastener of the new blade, and swivel the blade into engagement with the arm.

To remove the blade rubber depress the retaining pin on the outer end of the blade and slide the rubber out of the retainer clips.

Blade rubbers should be renewed each year.

Dynamo lubrication
Fig. 4
To lubricate the dynamo add a few drops of oil through the central hole in the rear bearing housing. Avoid overlubrication.

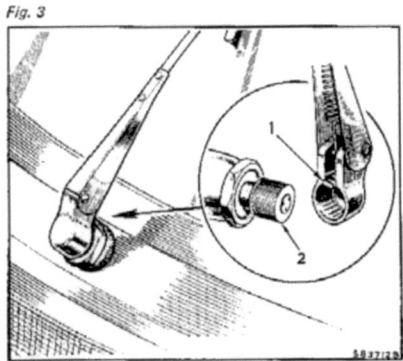
Fig. 3

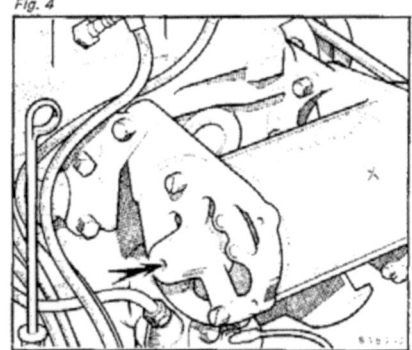
Fig. 4

Electrical

Headlamps
European type
Fig. 5 (inset)

To renew the headlamp bulb remove the screw from beneath the headlamp and withdraw the rim. Remove the three inner rim-retaining screws, remove the rim and pull the light unit forward from the back-shell.

The bulb is released by withdrawing the three-pin socket and pinching the two ends of the wire retaining clip to clear the bulb flange. When replacing the bulb ensure that the rectangular pip on the bulb flange engages the slot in the reflector seating. Replace the spring clip with its coils resting in the base of the bulb flange and engaging the two retaining lugs on the reflector seating for the bulb.

L.H.D. except Europe and North America
Fig. 5

Access to the bulb is obtained in the same manner as that described for European-type headlamps. Twist the back-shell anti-clockwise and pull it off. The bulb can then be withdrawn from its holder.

U.K. sealed-beam type
Fig. 6

To change a sealed-beam light unit remove the lamp rim by releasing the rim-retaining screw at the bottom of the rim assembly. Remove the three retaining screws securing the inner light rim and remove the rim assembly. Pull the unit forward and disconnect the three-pin socket to release it from the back-shell.

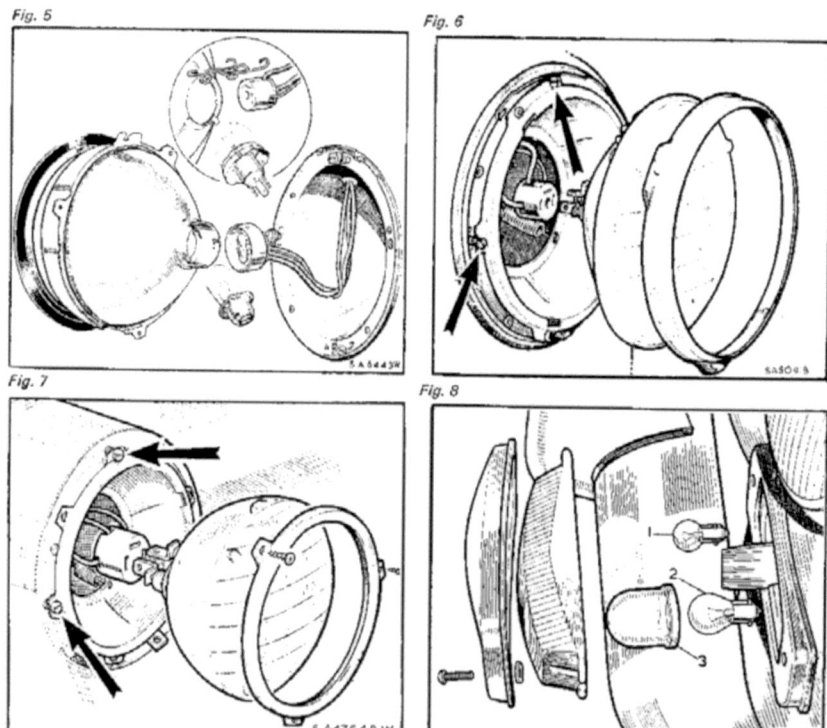

Fig. 5

Fig. 6

Fig. 7

Fig. 8

North American sealed-beam type
Fig. 7

To change a sealed-beam light unit remove the retaining screw from the bottom face of the lamp rim, and detach the rim. Slacken the three Phillips screws securing the light unit retaining rim and turn the rim anti-clockwise to remove, supporting the lens of the light unit at the same time. Pull the three-pin plug from the rear of the light unit.

Setting the headlight beams

The headlight beams must be set so that the main driving beams are straight ahead and parallel with the road surface and with each other, or in accordance with the local regulations. To adjust, remove the lamp rim and set each lamp to the correct position in the vertical plane by turning the adjusting screw at the top of the light unit in a clockwise direction to raise and anti-clockwise to lower the beam. Horizontal adjustment is made by turning the adjusting screw on the right-hand side of the light unit, on L.H.D. except Europe and North American type units two horizontal adjusting screws are fitted. The adjusting screws are indicated by arrows in Figs. 6 and 7.

Checking and resetting should be carried out at the beginning of each winter. This work is best entrusted to a Distributor/Dealer, who will have specialist equipment available for this purpose.

Side and direction indicator lamps
Fig. 8

Extract the two retaining screws to release the plated rim and the lens to gain access to both the light (1) and direction indicator (2) bulbs. An amber cover (3) is fitted over the direction indicator bulb when the vehicle is operating in countries where the lighting regulations require amber flashing indicators.

Stop, tail, and direction indicator lamps *Fig. 9*

Extract the one retaining screw from the bottom of the lamp and slide the lens upwards to release it from the retaining tongue at the top of the lamp.

Number-plate lamp
Fig. 10

The number-plate lamp is switched on with the sidelights and tail lights. Access to the bulbs (1) is obtained by unscrewing the one slotted screw and removing the domed cover (3) and glass (2).

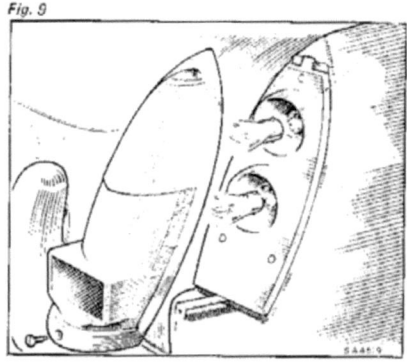
Fig. 9

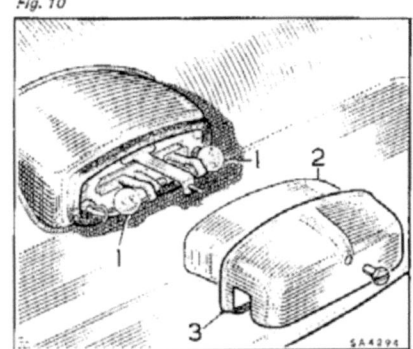
Fig. 10

Electrical

Panel and warning lights All the bulb holders are a push fit in the sockets and can be pulled from their fixtures at the back of the instrument panel to enable a defective bulb to be replaced.

Replacement bulbs

	Volts	Watts	BMC Part No.
Headlamp, L.H.D. (except North America and Europe)	12	50/40	BFS 415
Headlamps (Europe except France)	12	45/40	BFS 410
Headlamp (France only)	12	45/40	BFS 411
Sidelamp	12	4	BFS 222
Sidelamp, direction indicator (North America and Italy)	12	6/21	BFS 380
Direction indicator, front	12	21	BFS 382
Direction indicator, rear	12	21	BFS 382
Tail and stop lamp	12	6/21	BFS 380
Number-plate illumination lamp	12	6	BFS 989
Panel and warning lights	12	2·2	BFS 987

IGNITION

Static ignition timing The point where ignition should start is given in 'GENERAL DATA'. With the crankshaft stationary at this position the contact breaker points should be just beginning to open. When the engine is running timing is varied by a centrifugal advance mechanism.

Checking Fig. 1 The information given below describes a method of checking the ignition timing; it does not detail the resetting of the timing when the distributor has been removed from the engine.

Check that the contact points are set to the correct gap when on the peak of the distributor cam.

The rim of the crankshaft pulley has a small groove (1) which will correspond with the long pointer on the timing cover when Nos. 1 and 4 pistons are at T.D.C.; the other two pointers indicate 5° and 10° B.T.D.C. To turn the pulley to the required position, remove the sparking plugs, engage top gear, and push the car forward until the groove in the pulley is in the correct position (see 'GENERAL DATA').

With the crankshaft in this position the contact points should be just about to open. If the points are open, slacken the distributor clamp screw (2) and turn the distributor body in the direction of the arrow 'R' (anti-clockwise) until they are closed; if they are closed, turn the distributor in the direction of the arrow 'A' (clockwise). In both cases turn the distributor until the points are just parting. Tighten the distributor clamp screw.

A simple electrical method may be used to ensure accuracy. Connect a 12-volt bulb between the low-tension terminal on the side of the distributor and a good earth point on the engine. Switch on the ignition. If the bulb lights, slacken the clamp screw and turn the distributor in the direction of arrow 'R' until the light goes out and then back in the direction of 'A' until it just lights. This will give the correct static timing.

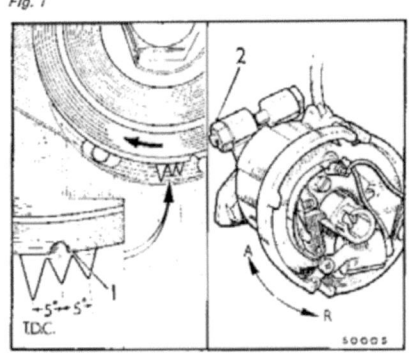

Fig. 1

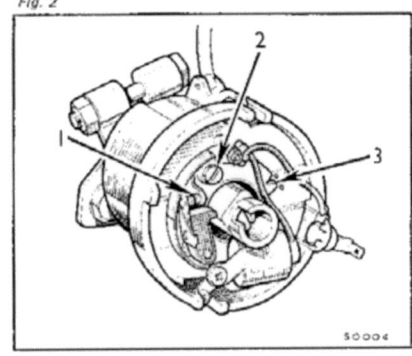

Fig. 2

Ignition

Distributor   Check the functioning of the automatic advance and retard mechanism as follows.

Centrifugal advance mechanism   Remove the distributor cap and grasp the rotor firmly. Turn the rotor arm in the direction of rotation and release it. The rotor arm should return to its original position without showing any tendency to stick.

Contact breaker
Fig. 2   Remove the distributor cap and turn the crankshaft until the contacts are fully open. Check the gap (1) with a feeler gauge (see **'GENERAL DATA'**); the gauge should be a sliding fit in the gap. If the gap varies appreciably from the gauge thickness, slacken the contact plate securing screw (2) and adjust the contact gap by inserting a screwdriver in the notched hole at the end of the plate (3) and turning clockwise to decrease and anti-clockwise to increase the gap. Retighten the securing screw.

If the contact breaker points are burned or blackened, clean them with a fine carborundum stone or with fine emery-cloth.

Cleaning the contacts is made easier if the contact breaker lever carrying the moving contact is removed. To do this unscrew the nut securing the end of the spring, remove the spring washer, flat washer, and both lead terminals, and lift off the lever complete with spring. After cleaning refit the contact breaker and check the gap.

Lubrication
Fig. 3   Remove the distributor cover and rotor arm and lightly smear the cam (1) and contact breaker pivot (2) with grease to Ref. B (page 52). Avoid overgreasing.

Drop a few spots of oil on to the automatic advance weights at (3) and on the screw (4) in the centre of the cam spindle after withdrawing the rotor arm. Do not remove this screw as clearance is provided for the oil to pass. Replace the rotor arm with its drive lug correctly engaging the spindle slot and push it onto the spindle as far as it will go.

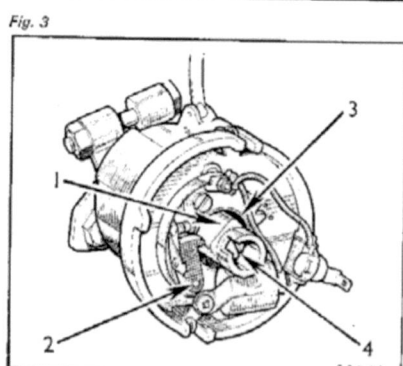
Fig. 3

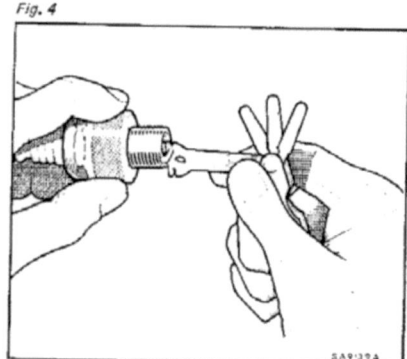
Fig. 4

Carefully wipe away all surplus oil and see that the contact breaker points are perfectly clean.

Ignition cables (high-tension) The high-tension cables connecting the distributor to the sparking plugs may, after long use, also show signs of perishing. They must then be replaced by the correct type of ignition cable. Cut the cables to length, fill the holes in the cap with silicone grease, push the cables well home in the cap, and secure with the pointed screws.

Sparking plugs
Fig. 4
The sparking plugs should be cleaned of all carbon deposit using a stiff brush dipped in paraffin (kerosene), or preferably with an air-blast service unit.

Check the plug gaps, and reset if necessary to the recommended gap (see **'GENERAL DATA'**). To reset, use a special Champion sparking plug gauge and setting tool; move the side electrode, never the centre one.

When refitting the plugs make sure that the copper washers are not defective in any way. If they have become worn and flattened, fit new ones to ensure a gas-tight joint. Screw the plug down by hand as far as possible, then use a spanner for tightening only. Always use a tubular box spanner to avoid possible damage to the insulator, and do not under any circumstances use a movable wrench. Never overtighten a plug, but ensure that a good joint is made between the plug body, washer, and cylinder head. Wipe clean the outside of the plugs before reconnecting the H.T. leads.

When fitting new sparking plugs ensure that only the recommended type and grade are used (see **'GENERAL DATA'**).

WIRING DIAGRAM

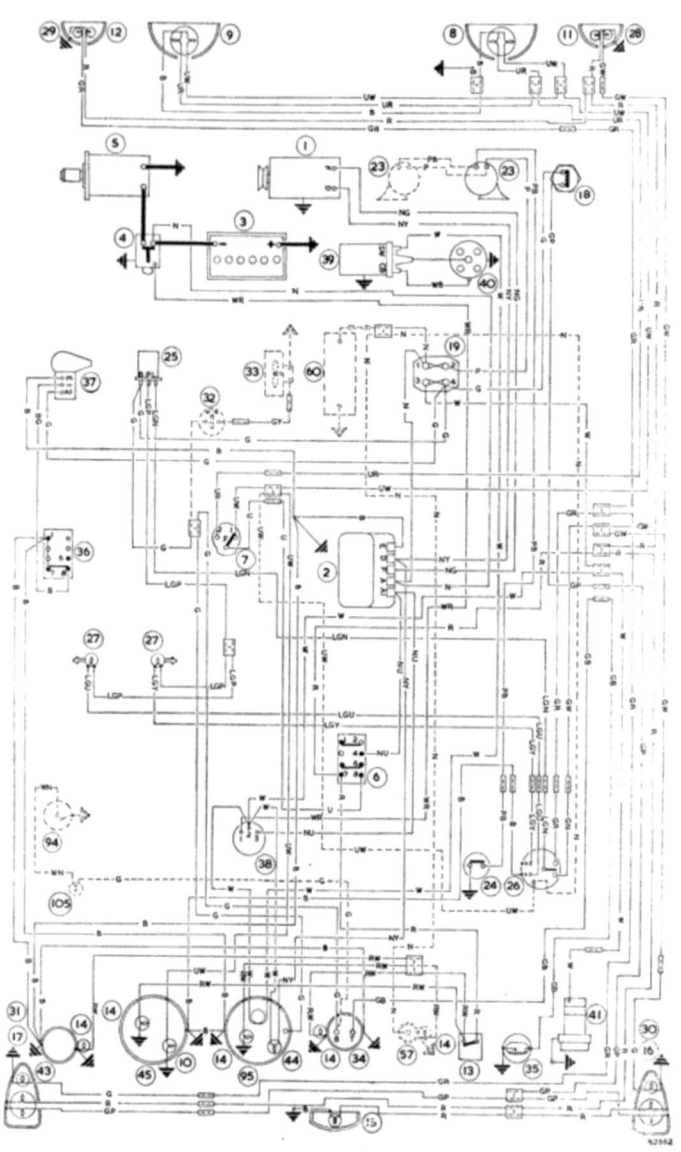

1. Dynamo.
2. Control box.
3. Battery (12-volt).
4. Starter solenoid.
5. Starter motor.
6. Lighting switch.
7. Headlight dip switch.
8. R.H. headlamp.
9. L.H. headlamp.
10. Main-beam warning light.
11. R.H. sidelamp.
12. L.H. sidelamp.
13. Panel light switch.
14. Panel lights.
15. Number-plate illumination lamp.
16. R.H. stop and tail lamp.
17. L.H. stop and tail lamp.
18. Stop light switch.
19. Fuse unit (35 amps.).
23. Horn (twin horns when fitted).
24. Horn-push.
25. Flasher unit.
26. Direction indicator switch (headlight flasher when fitted).
27. Direction indicator warning lights.
28. R.H. front flasher lamp.
29. L.H. front flasher lamp.
30. R.H. rear flasher lamp.
31. L.H. rear flasher lamp.
32. Heater or fresh-air motor switch (when fitted).
33. Heater or fresh-air motor (when fitted).
34. Fuel gauge.
35. Fuel gauge tank unit.
36. Windscreen wiper switch.
37. Windscreen wiper motor.
38. Ignition/starter switch.
39. Ignition coil.
40. Distributor.
41. Fuel pump.
43. Oil pressure gauge.
44. Ignition warning light.
45. Speedometer.
57. Cigar lighter (illuminated).
60. Radio.
94. Oil filter switch.
95. Tachometer (impulse type).
105. Oil filter warning light.

CABLE COLOUR CODE

N. Brown.   P. Purple.   W. White.
U. Blue.   G. Green.   Y. Yellow.
R. Red.   L.G. Light Green. B. Black.

When a cable has two colour code letters the first denotes the main colour and the second denotes the tracer colour.

ENGINE

Sump

Checking engine oil level
Fig. 1
The level of the oil in the engine sump is indicated by the dipstick (3) on the right-hand side of the engine. Maintain the level at the 'MAX' mark on the dipstick and never allow it to fall below the 'MIN' mark.

The filler (2) is on the forward end of the rocker cover and is provided with a quick-action cap. The filler cap also incorporates a filter for the closed-circuit crankcase breathing intake.

The oil level should always be checked before a long run.

Draining
Fig. 1
To drain the engine oil, remove the drain plug (1) located on the right-hand side at the rear of the sump. This operation should be carried out while the engine is warm.

Clean the drain plug; check that its copper sealing washer is in a satisfactory condition, and refit.

Filling
Fill the engine with the correct quantity (see **'GENERAL DATA'**) of oil to Ref. A (page 52). Run the engine for a short while then allow it to stand for a few minutes before checking the level with the dipstick.

Fig. 1
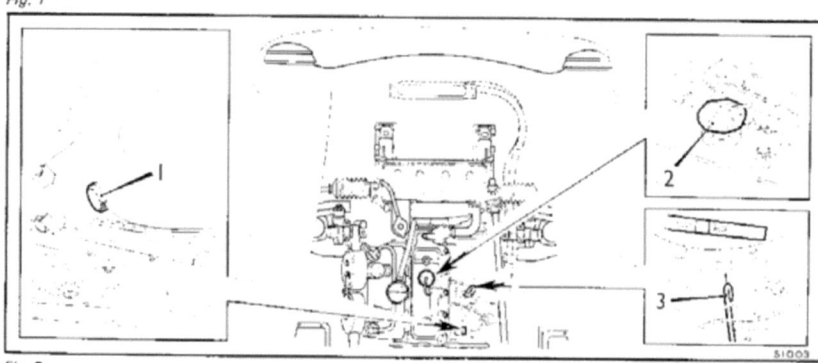

Fig. 2
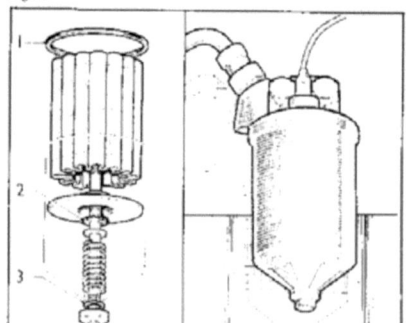

Fig. 3
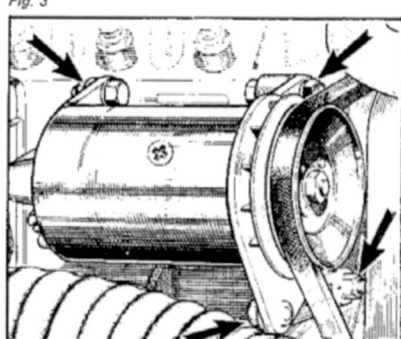

Oil filter
Fig. 2
The external oil filter is of the renewable-element type and is located on the right-hand side of the cylinder block. The filter is released by undoing the central bolt securing the filter body to the filter head. Wash out the casing with petrol (gasoline) and dry it before fitting a new element. Check that the sealing rings (1) and (3) and the rubber washer (2) are in a satisfactory condition. Reassemble the filter, ensuring that the components are correctly positioned.

Fan belt
Checking
When correctly tensioned, a deflection, under moderate hand pressure, of $\frac{1}{2}$ in. (13 mm.) approximately should be possible at the midway point of the longest belt run between the pulleys.

Adjusting
Fig. 3
To adjust the belt tension, slacken the dynamo securing bolts (arrowed), and move the dynamo to the required position, using only hand pressure. Avoid overtensioning. Tighten the securing bolts.

Valve rocker clearance
Checking
Fig. 4
Remove the rocker cover and insert a ·012 in. (·305 mm.) feeler gauge between the valve rocker arms and valve stems (inset). The gauge should be a sliding fit when the engine is cold. Check each clearance in the following order:

Check No. 1 valve with No. 8 fully open. Check No. 8 valve with No. 1 fully open.
,, ,, 3 ,, ,, ,, 6 ,, ,, ,, ,, 6 ,, ,, ,, 3 ,, ,,
,, ,, 5 ,, ,, ,, 4 ,, ,, ,, ,, 4 ,, ,, ,, 5 ,, ,,
,, ,, 2 ,, ,, ,, 7 ,, ,, ,, ,, 7 ,, ,, ,, 2 ,, ,,

Adjusting
Slacken the adjusting screw locknut on the opposite end of the rocker arm and rotate the screw clockwise to reduce the clearance or anti-clockwise to increase it. Retighten the locknut when the clearance is correct, holding the screw against rotation with a screwdriver.

Water pump lubrication
Fig. 5
To lubricate the water pump remove the screw plug (arrowed) in the pump casing and add a small quantity of one of the recommended greases.

Lubricate sparingly.

Fig. 4

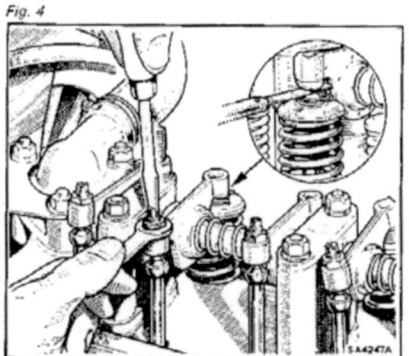

Fig. 5

Engine

Closed-circuit breathing
Oil filler cap
Fig. 6

An air filter is incorporated in the oil filler cap (1). The cap and filter are renewed only as a complete assembly.

Breather control valve

Testing. With the engine at normal operating temperature, run it at idling speed. Remove the oil filler cap. If the valve is functioning correctly the engine speed will rise by 150 or 200 r.p.m. as the cap is removed, the change in speed being audibly noticeable. If no change in speed occurs, service the valve as follows.

Servicing. Remove the spring clip (2) and dismantle the valve. Clean all metal parts with a solvent (trichlorethylene, fuel, etc.). If deposits are difficult to remove, immerse in boiling water before applying the solvent. Do not use an abrasive.

Clean the diaphragm (3) with detergent or methylated spirits.

Replace components showing signs of wear or damage.

Reassemble the valve, making sure the metering needle (4) is in the cruciform guides (5) and the diaphragm is seated correctly.

Carburetters
Lubrication
Fig. 7

Each damper reservoir must be topped up periodically with thin engine oil to Ref. E (page 52). **Under no circumstances should heavy-bodied lubricant be used.** Unscrew the damper cap, withdraw the damper, and top up the reservoir until the oil level (arrowed) is $\frac{1}{2}$ in. (12 mm.) above the top of the hollow piston rod. Push the damper assembly back into position and screw the cap firmly into the reservoir.

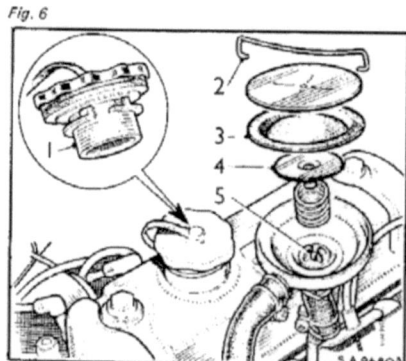

Fig. 6

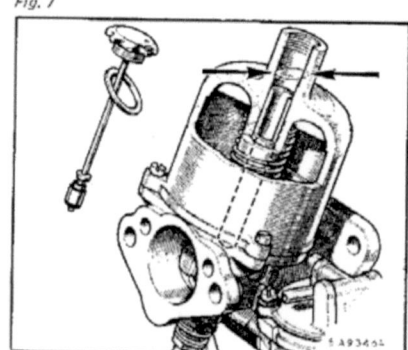

Fig. 7

Slow-running adjustment and synchronization
Fig. 8

When the engine is fully run in the slow running may require adjustment. This must only be carried out when the engine has reached its normal running temperature.

As the needle size is determined during engine development, tuning of the carburetters is confined to correct idling setting. Slacken the actuating arms on the throttle spindle interconnection. Close both throttles fully by unscrewing the throttle adjusting screws (1), then open each throttle by screwing down each screw one turn.

Remove the suction chamber (4) and piston assemblies, marking each to ensure replacement in their original positions, remove the air cleaners and disconnect the mixture control cable. Screw the jet adjusting nuts (2) until each jet is flush with the bridge of its carburetter, or as near to this as possible (both jets being in the same relative position to the bridge of their respective carburetters). Replace the pistons and suction chamber assemblies, and check that the pistons fall freely onto the bridge of the carburetters (by means of the piston lifting pins (3)). Turn down each jet adjusting nut two complete turns (12 flats).

Restart the engine, and turn the throttle adjusting screws to give the desired idling speed by moving each screw an equal amount. By listening to the hiss in the intakes, adjust the throttle adjusting screws until the intensity of the hiss is similar on both intakes. This will synchronize the throttles.

When this is satisfactory, the mixture should be adjusted by screwing each jet adjusting nut, up to weaken, or down to enrich by the same amount until the fastest idling speed consistent with even firing is obtained. During this adjustment it is necessary to press the jets upwards and ensure that they are in contact with the adjusting nuts.

As the mixture is adjusted the engine will probably run faster and it may therefore be necessary to unscrew the throttle adjusting screws a little, each by the same amount, to reduce the speed.

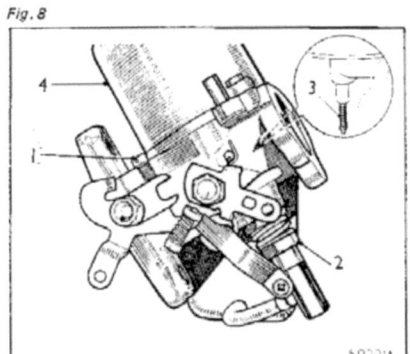

Fig. 8

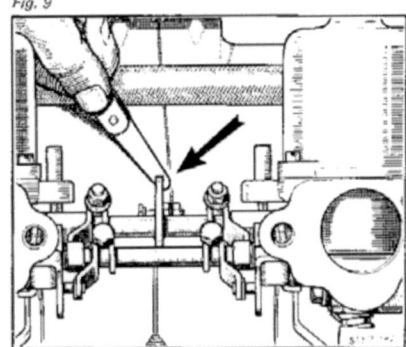

Fig. 9

Engine

Now check the mixture strength by lifting the piston of the front carburetter by approximately $\frac{1}{32}$ in. (·75 mm.) when:
  (1) If the engine speed increases, the mixture strength of the front carburetter is too rich.
  (2) If the engine speed immediately decreases, the mixture strength of the front carburetter is too weak.
  (3) If the engine speed momentarily increases very slightly, the mixture strength of the front carburetter is correct.

Repeat the operation at the rear carburetter, and after adjustment re-check the front carburetter, since both carburetters are interdependent.

When the mixture is correct the exhaust note should be regular and even. If it is irregular, with a splashy type of misfire and colourless exhaust, the mixture is too weak. If there is a regular or rhythmical type of misfire in the exhaust beat, together with a blackish exhaust, then the mixture is too rich.

Throttle linkage
Fig. 9
Each throttle is operated by a lever and pin, with the pin working in a forked lever attached to the throttle spindle. A clearance exists between the pin and fork which must be maintained when the throttle is closed and the engine idling to prevent any load from the accelerator linkage being transferred to the throttle butterfly and spindle.

To set this clearance, with the throttle shaft levers free on the throttle shaft, put a ·012 in. (·3 mm.) feeler between the throttle shaft stop at the top and the carburetter heat shield. Move the throttle shaft lever downwards until the lever pin rests lightly on the lower arm of the fork in the carburetter throttle lever. Tighten the clamp bolt of the throttle shaft lever at this position. When both carburetters have been dealt with, remove the feeler. The pins on the throttle shaft should then have clearance in the forks.

Reconnect the mixture control cable, ensuring that the jet heads return against the lower face of the jet adjusting nuts when the mixture control is pushed fully in. Pull out the mixture control knob on the dash panel until the linkage is about to move the carburetter jets a minimum of $\frac{1}{4}$ in. (6 mm.) and adjust the fast-idle adjusting screws to give an engine speed of about 1,000 r.p.m. when hot.

Air cleaners
The air cleaner covers and elements should only be removed when the elements are being renewed. To fit new elements, remove the interconnecting bracket securing nut and air cleaner bolts. Lift off the assemblies, remove the covers and extract the elements. Clean the containers thoroughly before fitting the new elements.

GEARBOX/REAR AXLE

Gearbox
Fig. 1
To gain access to the gearbox combined oil filler and level plug, lift the floor covering on the left-hand side of the gearbox cover and remove the rubber plug. Clean around the filler plug before removing it.

The oil level should be maintained at the bottom of the filler plug aperture threads.

Rear axle
Fig. 2
A combined oil filler and level plug is located on the rear of the axle. The oil level should be maintained at the bottom of the plug aperture; ensure that the car is standing level when checking. After topping up the oil level, allow sufficient time for any surplus oil, which may have been added accidentally, to run out of the aperture before replacing the plug.

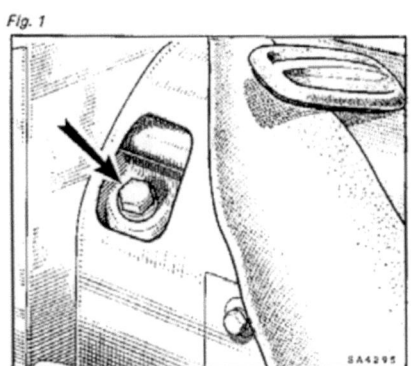
Fig. 1

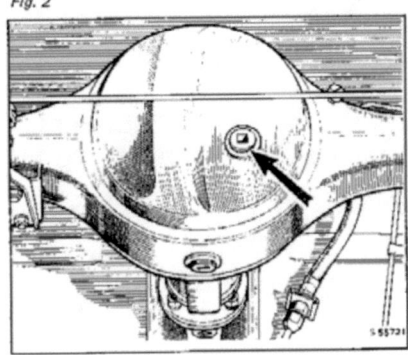
Fig. 2

STEERING/SUSPENSION

Lubrication
Steering rack
Fig. 1

A lubrication nipple for the steering rack is located on the left-hand side of the rack housing (right-hand side on left-hand drive cars), which is accessible when the bonnet is raised. When lubricating give a maximum of 10 strokes with an oil gun filled with one of the recommended oils.

Swivel axle pins
Fig. 2

Two lubricating nipples (1) and (2) are provided on each swivel pin. To lubricate, charge the nipples with one of the recommended greases. To ensure full penetration of the lubricant, this operation is best carried out with the car partly jacked up.

Steering connections
Fig. 2

The steering tie-rod ball joint at each side is provided with a lubrication nipple (3). To lubricate, charge the nipples with one of the recommended greases.

Front suspension outer fulcrum pins
Fig. 2

A lubricating nipple (4) is provided on each of the outer fulcrum pins. To lubricate, charge the nipples with one of the recommended greases.

Front wheel alignment

Incorrect front wheel alignment can cause excessive and uneven tyre wear. The front wheels must be set parallel or toe-in ⅛ in. (3·2 mm.) to each other when the steering is in the straight-ahead position.

To set the wheel alignment correctly requires the use of a special gauge; this work should be entrusted to your Distributor or Dealer.

Fig. 1

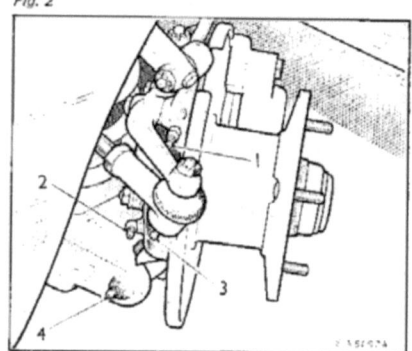

Fig. 2

GENERAL DATA

Engine	Engine type	12CC (4-cylinder overhead valve)
	Bore	2·78 in. (70·61 mm.)
	Stroke	3·2 in. (81·28 mm.)
	Cubic capacity	77·53 cu. in. (1275 c.c.)
	Compression ratio	8·8 : 1 or 8·0 : 1
	Firing order	1, 3, 4, 2
	Valve rocker clearance (cold)	·012 in. (·3 mm.)
	Idling setting	700 r.p.m. (hot)
	Oil pressure:	
	Normal (approx.)	40 to 70 lb./sq. in. (2·81 to 4·92 kg./cm.²)
	Idling (approx.)	20 lb./sq. in. (1·4 kg./cm.²)
Ignition	Sparking plugs	Champion UN12Y
	Sparking plug gap	·024 to ·026 in. (·62 to ·66 mm.)
	Static ignition timing:	
	High compression	7° B.T.D.C.
	Low compression	7° B.T.D.C.
	Stroboscopic ignition timing	22° at 1,000 r.p.m.
	Contact breaker gap	·014 to ·016 in. (·35 to ·38 mm.)
Fuel system	Carburetters	Twin S.U. type HS2
	Carburetter needles	Standard AN, Weak GG, Rich H6
	Spring	Light blue
	Pump	S.U. (Electric) type AUF 206
Transmission	Rear axle ratio	4·22 : 1
	Overall gear ratios: First	13·504 : 1
	With Second	8·085 : 1
	synchromesh Third	5·726 : 1
	Fourth	4·22 : 1
	Reverse	17·395 : 1
Wheels and tyres	Wheel size	Disc—3·5D × 13; wire—4J × 13
	Tyre size and type	5·20—13 Dunlop C41 Gold Seal (Nylon) Tubeless
		5·20—13 Heavy-Duty (6 ply) Tubeless
		145—13 SP41—Tubed

Tyre pressures (set cold):

	Dunlop C41 Gold Seal (Nylon); Heavy Duty	SP41
Normal:		
Front	18 lb./sq. in. (1·3 kg./cm.²)	22 lb./sq. in. (1·6 kg./cm.²)
Rear	20 lb./sq. in. (1·4 kg./cm.²)	24 lb./sq. in. (1·7 kg./cm.²)
For sustained speeds in excess of 80–85 m.p.h. (129–137 km.p.h.):		
Front	22 lb./sq. in. (1·6 kg./cm.²)	22 lb./sq. in. (1·6 kg./cm.²)
Rear	24 lb./sq. in. (1·7 kg./cm.²)	24 lb./sq. in. (1·7 kg./cm.²)

Dimensions		Wire wheels	Disc wheels
Track: Front		3 ft. 10$\frac{4}{16}$ in. (1·16 m.)	3 ft. 10$\frac{8}{16}$ in. (1·16 m.)
Rear		3 ft. 9¼ in. (1·15 m.)	3 ft. 8¾ in. (1·14 m.)
Turning circle: Left lock		32 ft. 1½ in. (9·79 m.)	
Right lock		31 ft. 2½ in. (9·51 m.)	
Front wheel alignment		Parallel to ⅛ in. toe-in (0 to 3·2 mm.)	
Wheelbase		6 ft. 8 in. (2·03 m.)	
Overall length		11 ft. 5⅜ in. (3·49 m.)	
Overall width: Disc wheels		4 ft. 6⅞ in. (1·4 m.)	
Wire wheels		4 ft. 8½ in. (1·5 m.)	
Overall height		4 ft. ⅜ in. (1·22 m.)	
Ground clearance		5 in. (12·7 cm.)	

Weight Dry weight .. .. 1,510 lb. (685 kg.)

Capacities
Fuel tank .. .. .. 6 gallons (7·2 U.S. gallons, 27·3 litres)
Engine sump (including filter) .. 6½ pints (7·8 U.S. pints, 3·7 litres)
Gearbox .. .. .. 2¼ pints (2·7 U.S. pints, 1·3 litres)
Rear axle .. .. .. 1¾ pints (2·1 U.S. pints, ·99 litre)
Cooling system (without heater) .. 10 pints (12 U.S. pints, 5·68 litres)
Heater .. .. .. ½ pint (·6 U.S. pint, ·25 litre)

MAINTENANCE SUMMARY

Detailed maintenance instructions will be found on the page given in brackets after each item.

Every week or before a long journey
Inspect engine oil level, and top up as necessary. (36)
Check water level in radiator, and top up if necessary. (19)
Check battery and top up to correct levels. (26)
Test tyre pressures. (22)

	Every 3,000 miles (5000 km.) or 3 months	Every 6,000 miles (10000 km.) or 6 months	Every 12,000 miles (20000 km.) or 12 months
Engine			
Top up carburetter piston dampers. (38)	X		
Check water level in radiator, and top up if necessary. (19)	X		
Check fan belt tension. (37)		X	
Check valve rocker clearances, and adjust if necessary. (37)		X	
Fit new air cleaner elements. (40)		X	X
Crankcase closed-circuit breathing system; change engine oil filler cap, test and clean crankcase breather valve. (38)			X
Top up windscreen washer bottle.	X	X	X
Ignition			
Check functioning of automatic advance and retard mechanism. (32)		X	X
Check, and adjust if necessary, distributor contact points. (32)		X	X
Lubricate all parts as necessary. (32)			X
Fit new sparking plugs. (33)			X
Clean and adjust sparking plugs. (33)		X	
Steering			
Check steering and suspension moving parts for wear.*		X	X
Check wheel alignment, and adjust if necessary. (42)*			X
Clutch			
Check level of fluid in hydraulic clutch supply tank, and top up if necessary. (24)	X	X	X

46

Brakes
Check brakes, and adjust if necessary. (24)
Make visual inspection of brake lines and pipes. (25)
Check level of fluid in the hydraulic supply tank, and top up if necessary. (24)
Inspect disc brake friction pads and report if attention is required. (25)*
Inspect and blow out brake linings and drums.*

General
Check rear road spring seat bolts.

Electrical
Check battery cell specific gravity readings and top up to correct levels. (26)*
Check all lamps for correct functioning.
Check headlamp alignment. (29)

Lubrication
Check and top up engine oil level. (36)
Lubricate all grease nipples (except steering rack and pinion). (51)
Change engine oil (if using monograde only). (36)
Top up oil level in gearbox and rear axle. (41)
Fit new oil filter element. (37)
Change oil in engine. (36)
Lubricate dynamo bearing. (27)
Lubricate all grease nipples. (51)
Lubricate water pump sparingly. (37)
Lubricate steering rack and pinion. (42)
Lubricate door locks and hinges.

Wheels and tyres
Check tyre pressures. (22)

* These items should be entrusted to your Distributor or Dealer.

NOTE.—Take the advice of your Distributor/Dealer on:
1. The need for more frequent engine oil changes;
2. When to change round wheels;
3. When to check and adjust headlight beams.

47

BMC SERVICE

Identification When communicating with your Distributor or Dealer always quote the car and engine numbers. When the communication concerns the transmission units or body details it is necessary to quote also the transmission casing and body numbers.

Car number. Stamped on a plate secured to the left-hand inner wheel arch, under the bonnet.

Engine number. Stamped on a plate secured to the right-hand side of the cylinder block.

Gearbox number. Stamped on the left-hand side of the gearbox casing.

Rear axle number. Stamped on the front of the left-hand rear axle tube near the spring seating.

Warranty By keeping the Passport to Service, signed by the Distributor, Dealer, or vendor in the vehicle, you can quickly establish the date of purchase and provide the necessary details if adjustments are required to be carried out under warranty.

Claims for the replacement of parts under warranty must be submitted to the supplying Distributor or Dealer or, when this is not possible, to the nearest Distributor or Dealer, informing them of the vendor's name and address. Except in cases of emergency warranty work should always be carried out by a BMC appointed Distributor or Dealer.

Service Parts When Service Parts are required insist on BMC GENUINE PARTS as these are designed and tested for your vehicle and in addition have the full backing of the BMC Factory Warranty. ONLY WHEN GENUINE PARTS ARE USED CAN BMC ACCEPT RESPONSIBILITY.

All BMC GENUINE PARTS and APPROVED ACCESSORIES can be identified by this label on the packing.

Factory Exchange Unit Scheme

The BMC Exchange Scheme—the most comprehensive in Europe—has been designed specifically to **save you money**.

Briefly, the scheme covers practically every major assembly on any BMC car marketed in the last 10 years, and includes components such as heaters and servo units for brakes as well as a wide range of instruments.

If, for example, you want another engine, the Distributor returns the old one to us, and we issue one which has been fully reconditioned in one of our own specialist factories.

By using this technique the cost is considerably reduced but **not the quality**, and each replacement unit carries the same factory warranty as a brand-new one.

Your BMC Distributor or Dealer will be pleased to give you full details and comparative examples of the money which you can save by taking advantage of this scheme.

Units available

- Engines and Ancillaries
- Clutches
- Gearboxes
- Rear Axles and Differential Assemblies
- Braking System Units
- Steering Gears
- Instruments
- Electrical Units
- Bumper Bars
- Fuel Pumps
- Shock Absorbers
- Heaters

Supplementary tool kit

To supplement the tool kit a waterproof canvas roll containing the following is obtainable from all Distributors. Part No. AKF 1596 should be quoted.

6 spanners: $\frac{3}{8}$ in. $\times \frac{3}{8}$ in. A.F.
$\frac{7}{16}$ in. $\times \frac{1}{2}$ in. A.F.
$\frac{1}{2}$ in. $\times \frac{9}{16}$ in. A.F.
$\frac{9}{16}$ in. $\times \frac{5}{8}$ in. A.F.
$\frac{11}{16}$ in. $\times \frac{13}{16}$ in. A.F.
$\frac{3}{4}$ in. $\times \frac{7}{8}$ in. A.F.

1 pair 6 in. pliers.
1 7 in. $\times \frac{3}{8}$ in. diameter tommy-bar.
1 $\frac{1}{2}$ in. $\times \frac{9}{16}$ in. A.F. tubular spanner.
2 screwdrivers.

BMC SERVICE LIMITED
a Subsidiary of The British Motor Corporation Limited
COWLEY · OXFORD · ENGLAND

Telephone: Oxford 77777 *Telegrams:* BMCSERV. Telex. Oxford
Telex: BMCSERV. Oxford 83145 and 83146
Overseas Cables: BMCSERV. Telex. Oxford. England

LUBRICATION

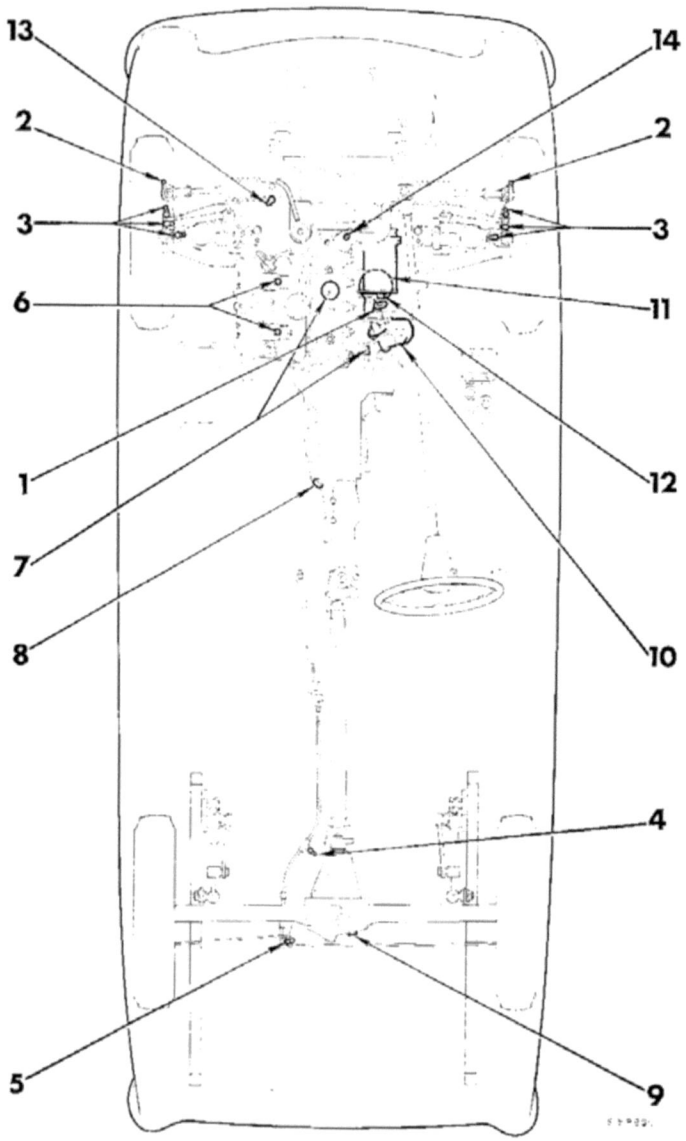

WEEKLY

(1) ENGINE. Check the oil level, and top up as necessary with oil to Ref. A.

Every 3,000 miles (500 km.) or 3 months

(2) STEERING TIE-ROD BALL JOINT (2 nipples). Give three or four strokes of a gun filled with grease to Ref. C.

(3) SWIVEL AXLES AND SUSPENSION LOWER JOINTS (6 nipples). Give three or four strokes of a gun filled with grease to Ref. C.

(4) HAND BRAKE CABLE (1 nipple). Give three or four strokes of a gun filled with grease to Ref. C.

(5) HAND BRAKE COMPENSATOR LEVER (1 nipple). Give three or four strokes of a gun filled with grease to Ref. C.

(6) CARBURETTERS. Top up damper assembly reservoirs with oil to Ref. E.

(7) ENGINE (if using monograde or single-viscosity oils only). Drain, and refill with fresh oil.

Every 6,000 miles (10000 km.) or 6 months

(7) ENGINE. Drain, and refill with fresh oil to Ref. A.

(8) GEARBOX. Check the oil level, and top up if necessary with oil to Ref. A.

(9) REAR AXLE. Check the oil level, and top up if necessary with oil to Ref. B.

(10) DISTRIBUTOR. Lubricate all parts as necessary.

(11) OIL FILTER. Wash the bowl in fuel and fit a new element.

(12) DYNAMO. Add a few drops of oil to Ref. A through the oil hole in the commutator end bearing.

Every 12,000 miles (20000 km.) or 12 months

(13) STEERING-RACK. Apply a gun filled with oil to Ref. B to the nipple on the steering-rack and give 10 strokes only.

(14) WATER PUMP. Remove the plug and add grease to Ref. C; replace the plug.

Lubrication

KEY TO RECOMMENDED LUBRICANTS

Component	A — Engine and Gearbox			B — Rear Axle and Steering Gear		C — All Grease Points	D — Upper Cylinder Lubricant	E — Oilcan and Carburetter
Climatic conditions predominating	Tropical and temperate down to 5° C. (41° F.)	Extreme cold, temperatures between 5° C. (41° F.) and −12° C. (10° F.)	Arctic conditions, temperatures consistently below −12° C. (10° F.)	All conditions down to −12° C. (10° F.)	Arctic, consistently below −12° C. (10° F.)			
DUCKHAM'S	Q.20/50	Q.5500 Q.20/50	Q.5500	Duckham's Hypoid 90	Duckham's Hypoid 80	Duckham's L.B.10 Grease	Duckham's Adcoid Liquid	Q.5500
CASTROL	Castrol XL	Castrolite	Castrol Z	Castrol Hypoy	Castrol Hypoy Light	Castrolease L.M.	Castrollo	Castrolite
STERNOL	W.W. 40	W.W. Multi-grade 10W/40	W.W. 10	Ambroleum E.P. 90	Ambroleum E.P. 80	Sternoline L.H.T.	Sternol Magikoyl	W.W. Multi-grade 10W/40
MOBIL	Mobiloil A.F.* Mobiloil Special 20W/40	Mobiloil Special 10W/30	Mobiloil 10W	Mobilube G.X. 90	Mobilube G.X. 80	Mobilgrease M.P.	Mobil Upperlube	Mobiloil Special 10W/30
ESSO	Esso Motor Oil 40/50† Esso Motor Oil 40 Esso Extra Motor Oil 20W/40	Esso Motor Oil 20W/30† Esso Motor Oil 20 Esso Extra Motor Oil	Esso Motor Oil 10W Esso Extra Motor Oil 5W/20	Esso Gear Oil G.P. 90/140† or G.P. 90	Esso Gear Oil G.P. 80	Esso Multipurpose Grease H	Esso Upper Cylinder Lubricant	Esso Extra Motor Oil
FILTRATE	Filtrate Heavy Filtrate 20W/50	Filtrate 10W/30 Filtrate Zero	Filtrate Sub Zero 10W	Filtrate Hypoid Gear 90	Filtrate Hypoid Gear 80	Filtrate Super Lithium Grease	Filtrate Petroyle	Filtrate 10W/30
BP	Energol S.A.E. 40	Energol S.A.E. 20W Super Visco-Static† Visco-Static*	Energol S.A.E. 10W Super Visco-Static† Visco-Static*	Gear Oil S.A.E. 90 E.P.	Gear Oil S.A.E. 80 E.P.	Energrease L. 2	Upper Cylinder Lubricant	Visco-Static* or Super Visco-Static†
SHELL	Shell Super Motor Oil Shell X-100 40 Shell X-100 Multigrade 20W/40*	Shell Super Motor Oil Shell X-100 20W Shell X-100 Multigrade 10W/30*	Shell Super Motor Oil Shell X-100 10W Shell X-100 Multigrade 10W/30*	Shell Spirax 90 E.P.	Shell Spirax 80 E.P.	Shell Retinax A	Shell Upper Cylinder Lubricant	Shell Super Motor Oil

* Not available in the United Kingdom.   † Available in the United Kingdom only.